FOREWARD

As an attorney working at Community Legal Services where we provide free, civil legal services to low-income Philadelphians, I am witness to the daily struggles of the city's poorest families and individuals. For these families, issues of poverty, mental and physical health, race, and trauma become inextricably intertwined. Although many people and groups will tell us that we now live in a post-racial society where opportunities have been equalized for women and people of color, the ever-increasing gaps in poverty and achievement between communities of color and their white counterparts will tell us otherwise.

In Philadelphia, named the poorest major city in the country in 2014 with a deep-poverty rate of 12.2 percent (almost twice the national deep-poverty rate of 6.3 percent), the Public Health Department reported last year in its Community Health Assessment that "racial/ethnic disparities are evident across a range of health issues."

African Americans, for instance, experienced disproportionately poor health in many areas including:
- Literacy
- Unemployment
- Life expectancy
- Premature death
- Adult smoking
- Smoking deaths
- Secondhand smoke exposure
- Child and adult obesity
- Youth sugary drink consumption

- Hypertension
- Child asthma hospitalization
- Elevated lead levels
- Child mortality
- Homicide mortality
- Firearm homicides
- Low access to healthy foods and recreational facilities.

Similarly, the Hispanic community experienced the poorest health in the following areas:
- Reading ability in 3rd grade
- High school graduation
- Unemployment
- Poverty
- Child obesity
- Adult sugary drink consumption
- Teen births
- Lack of insurance among children and adults
- Access to care
- Adult and teen mental health.

There was limited data on the Asian community. These social, physical, mental, and behavioral health issues are all inter-related to exposure to trauma. It becomes a vicious cycle that feeds upon itself.

These statistics are more than just numbers, however. Part of the reason why cycles of poverty and trauma perpetuate and repeat is because the stories behind the statistics are rendered invisible, go unacknowledged, or are manipulated to suit particular agendas. When our stories and our truths go untold and unshared, the cycles of trauma are bound to repeat, with no space or time given to evaluate one's journey and shift course.

As a Black woman standing at the intersections of race, class, and gender, I am also intimately familiar with the stories behind these statistics. Like the editors of this book, I am connected to these stories because I recognize myself in the words and experiences of these survivors, as a survivor of trauma and mental illness myself. And we not only see ourselves reflected in these stories - we see our mothers and our fathers, our sisters and our brothers, our neighbors and our friends. We understand intuitively that working with survivors of trauma not only allows our clients to access mechanisms for healing, but that this work extends beyond the individual to begin to reverse the vicious and destructive cycles that our communities have fallen into due to institutions which systematically deny the right to

The Color of Hope:

People of Color Mental Health Narratives

Edited By

Vanessa Hazzard & Iresha Picot, M.Ed

Foreward By

Rasheedah Phillips, Esq.

ISBN: 1514273489
ISBN-13: 978-1514273487

life, liberty, justice, shelter, service, and good health.

Theories of epigenetics suggest that there are particular genetic traits that pass down trans-generationally. These traits, depending on certain triggers in an environment, can switch on or off, catalyzing certain behaviors in a micro-system (such as a cell) or a macro-system (a person's behavioral traits). In much the same way that DNA is encoded in us, it is posited that we also inherit our ancestral memories; when ancestral memory is triggered in an individual, the memories may directly impact their health, psychology, or behavior. Theoretical physicist Alberto Hernando deCastro uses the laws of physics to study the ways in which communities retain memories, finding a time-based, underlying logic in how communities develop and interact, with a city's growth being largely dependent on factors in the city's past. Such research is useful in understanding how trauma and the post-traumatic stress can connect or disconnect us from our pasts, and the ways in which human behavior, in the aggregate, can influence an entire community or city, or how historical events, such as slavery or war, transform our communities in such a way that it displaces us completely from those events and its sources.

To create change we must all work together to dismantle the cycles of trauma. We will not do this alone. We will not be ashamed. We will hold each other up and echo each other's troubles because we did not come here alone, systematic oppression has always haunted our futures. It is up to us to change the paradigm and cultivate practical methods of healing. Telling our stories and speaking our truths allows us to practically explore the ways in which our collective and personal pasts continues to affect us. It also effects how we reinforce or manifest negative and positive cycles of experience, both in our personal lives as well as within the larger communities and societies that we participate in, and how we can break or shift these cycles. We must educate ourselves and share sustainable solutions to breaking cycles of trauma. This book contains the truth, words, hopes, dreams, lessons, experiences, wisdom, and stories of those who are best positioned to speak on it and identify the solutions: the victims and survivors of trauma themselves.

-Rasheedah Phillips, Esq.

PREFACE: IRESHA PICOT

"I ain't going to sit in no white person's face". Those were the words my childhood friend said to me one day about ten years ago, when I begged her to go and seek out professional therapy for the sexual trauma she experienced as a child. Her words echoed so many in our community, who have went through similar passages of trauma, but viewed the therapeutic process as inherently distrustful, Eurocentric and foreign.
I grew up under the Mason Dixon line, where you turned to God, and not a therapist, when you wanted to lift up those scary burdens that rested on your soul. God would take care of all things. How many times have we heard the scripture "Give your burdens to the Lord, and he will take care of you" (Psalms 55:22). The church was the only time where people could come and lay those burdens down. You didn't tell a therapist about the neighbor touching you as a child, or the physical abuse you suffered in your home. Those were secrets you dared not air out to the world, and if you told anyone, you told the church through testimony, praise and worship. The thought of sitting down in front of someone, telling your problems, were a complete "no-no". God and the Church was the alpha and the omega towards recovery and resiliency.

As I became a Therapist many years later, I often thought about all of the people who I knew as an adolescent who suffered in silence; because telling someone of your 'problems' was considered complaining. *The Color of Hope* is a book for those who have never had the safe space to talk about their mental health issues. Who may or may not have been able to access mental health places to bear witness to their pain. This book will hold space for their voices and the many more in the black and brown communities who suffer in silence without a space to free themselves up from their everyday pain. My goal with *The Color of Hope* is to break the stigma in our communities surrounding the secrecy of speaking your pain into existence. There is power in telling your story.

-Iresha Picot

PREFACE: VANESSA HAZZARD

Not long ago, while taking out the trash to the alley behind our house, my brother found a woman's lifeless body. He told me about the incident later when I got home and how the passerby and first responders treated her like another poor, random, black body found next to a pile of garbage. My brother said she was wearing a hospital bracelet. I asked what her name was, though a part of me already knew. He confirmed my suspicion and I was immediately filled with emotion.

In 2013, after being released from the mood disorder wing of a mental health facility, I attended a partial hospitalization program. There, I met a woman about twenty-five years my elder, who attended the long-term care program. She happened to live in one of the houses directly behind me. On the van rides to the treatment facility, we talked about our love of baking cookies with our children and grandchildren. It was her body that was found in the alley. I felt guilty that I didn't keep in touch with her after the program. I felt sad for her grandkids that they would never bake with her again. Being that I am a brown woman living with bipolar disorder and PTSD, I see myself in the faces of those society often ridicules or ignores. I couldn't help but think if that would be me in twenty years…just another dead "crazy person".

The Color of Hope is about my neighbor and those like her. This book gives a voice to the silent battles faced when living with mental illness. Shame, avoidance, fear, and other-ism are concepts associated with mental illness in the general population yet it seems to be amplified in communities of color. True healing can take place only when we are willing to see what lies before us. De-stigmatizing mental illness aids in that process.

Reading through the submissions we received for this book, I was incredibly moved by the experiences of our contributors. They represent those living with or affected by loved ones with depression, bipolar disorder, borderline personality disorder, post-traumatic stress disorder, schizophrenia, and other conditions. They are men and women, children and adults, political prisoners, college students, politicians, musicians, business people, artists, fathers, mothers, daughters...all of African, Latino, and Asian descent. Their narratives add to the tapestry of the human experience and without them, our history is incomplete.

-Vanessa Hazzard

Please be warned.
Some stories may be triggering for those that struggle with self-harm or suicidal ideation. While this book is intended to genuinely share the experiences of others, we do not in any way wish to romanticize poor coping mechanisms. Please contact your healthcare provider or call 911 if you are in need of help.

CONTENTS

ACKNOWLEDGMENTS

A special thanks to:

Orneno Wright of Aje Book Consulting

All of our contributors, for being so brave and willing to share their stories with the world.

To all of you, for bearing witness to the lives of those living with mental illness.

Brianna's Poem

I think my bucket is half full.
I do fill a lot of buckets.
I think I can fill someone's bucket by giving them a hi-five or inviting them
to eat lunch with me.
I think all buckets should be filled.
None should be empty.
Everyone has a bucket so it should be full.
I can help when I show I care.
I can stand up for people or share a snack.

-Brianna Kirkland, *Daughter of Lydia Kirkland, contributor to The Color of Hope.*
November 21, 1999- February 24, 2013

THE PATIENT PRISONER
BY MAURICE STEVENS

I've been told that I am sick,
Yeah,
Sicker than the illest patient.
'Cause with patience I ease into this dis-ease that is prison.
Mentally gifted to a give a mental uplifting,
So, gifted I listen to the mentally midget.
And because my mental inhibits a selfish decision,
I think for us.
I am the patient prisoner,
He/She who has self-sacrificed to satisfy thine own appetite,
And now full,
I thirst to make clear all the wrongs of what's right,
And all the rights of what's wrong.
So if you will, I ask your hand and that you partner
In this song,
Rule 1: Balance
Rule 2: Rhythm
Rule 3: Let go, and allow your body to give what's been given.
Off track it seems, I know, but all things come full circle,
See, in defense, we speak in circles sure not to let the next man get to
you.
Then he can't show you up, not beat you down,
When he can't find what's of things you've found,
 Nor the why fors.
When then knowing you become a thing they can only hope for.
So they believe what you show them,

As you must believe it to throw them
Touche Mr. Dunbar, we're still wearing the mask.
See,
Time doesn't really change things in knowing man's need for what's
passed.
So it's only because those around me are, that I'm sick,
It's a culture hood of the criminal minded, take your pick,
And find that here is but one of our psycho therapies, micro schemes,
Leading to macro means,
Where dreams are chased off by woe its me's
And it is on these that we lean,
As staff misinterprets our fiend,
Saying that it's only situational stressors,
So we stop trying to find time,
And learn to make it—design,
In brotherhood, the power of family we lecture.
With vow never to return,
But as promises break, vows burn,
We're recidivist, speaking everything but our truth,
It's this fear of failure that drives,
The honey bee back to its hive,
Where they lie of the outside to our youth,
So this truth, I will send,
As sentiment before I end,
A seed planted that I'll leave for you to nurture,
For as poetry reveals the poet,
And long suffering the stoic,
Work is conjured firth for the worker.
Prison robs the human being, from inception to cessation,
I stand an attestation,
It strips you, "Strip" stated as a triple entendre
For the physical, mental, and spiritual genres
But as prison takes it too allows one to find
this, of life's balance in agreement with time.
So when told I was sick, I agreed, then obliged
And it's within their diagnosis that I found man's need for the lie.
So yes, I am the patient prisoner.

Maurice Stevens is a Poet, Author, Playwright and Entrepreneur. He's also a member of Living on Vital Emotion writers group, which believes that: "In striving for growth, evolution one must never claim to know what they think, nor claim to think what

they know." Words that he lives by.
Maurice is a native of Philadelphia, PA and is currently incarcerate din the
Pennsylvania State Correctional system, S.C.I. Fayette. His forthcoming work will
include "Clipped Wings" and "Still Walking", books of poetry as well as a play
entitled: "Corner Boy".
Maurice can be contacted at:
Maurice Stevens
#KF-4856
P.O. Box 999
50 Overlook Drive
LaBelle, PA 15450

CLOSE TO HAPPY
BY YOLANDA AYESHA

I live in two worlds
Wonderland & The Real
It's so easy to forget
who u really are in The Real
White men in white coats
stick & probe
Telling me I have this dis-ease & that dis-ease
Then ask me if I'm blue
No, I'm more like grey
not this modern "grey is the new black" kind of grey
More like the color of the sky before a storm
Massive, burdensome, impermeable
This shits heavy
& at times it hurts
But I put on my best ruby woo smile & tell them "No" that "I'm just fine."
Before I can make it out of the office
my mother calls
Worried & anxious she asks,
"how was ur appointment ?"
So I tell her what I think she wishes were truths
"Fine"
"What's the matter? How do u feel?"
"Nothing's wrong ma, I'm ok"
All of my friends are too busy

off traveling the world
Or getting married
Or making babies
So I lay down & close my eyes to leave them all here in The Real
As I escape to Wonderland
Where I really am blue
Like the sky after a storm
Vast, limitless, luminous
Here, This shit is beautiful
Here, I'm beautiful...& free
Free to dance
Free to fly
Free to love
In wonderland the only probing & sticking done,
is between lovers
& mothers breathe easy having not forgotten
that here in Wonderland we're all Created in His image
She know Jah make no mistakes
So she rests calmly in the solace that
all her babies are happy, healthy & safe
Rested & rejuvenated my body begins to stir
as angels sweetly whisper their good morning song to me
It's time to return to The Real
So I rise
Shower
Dress
Swallow pills the white coats say will keep me here longer
& paint on my ruby roo smile to head out into The Real
I hear birds sweetly singing the angels song
& I smile
Maybe it's not so bad here after all
Living in The Real
I carry Wonderland in my heart
So that I'm always close to happy
& while I'm here, if ever I start to forget who I am
I just close my eyes
& wait for the angels to whisper their song

INTERVIEW WITH TAJSHA LEWIS

Vanessa: Hey Tajsha! Thanks so much for participating in this project. I know you have been living with mental illness for some time. What is your specific diagnosis?

Tajsha: In 2006 or 2007, I was diagnosed with bipolar disorder type II, progressing towards schizophrenia. I don't stay on meds very long so I'm feeling like schizophrenia is imminent.

Vanessa: How many times have you been hospitalized?

Tajsha: I've been hospitalized twice. The first time I wasn't very receptive to treatment so I signed myself out after 72 hours. The second time was different. I was ready to get better. Since then, I've begun to recognize that it (the illness) is a part of me. Overall I've been well, although I do have my moments.

Vanessa: Does mental illness run in your family?

Tajsha: Yes. My grandmother on my mom's side has schizophrenia. Her sister, my great aunt, killed herself by overdosing on sleeping pills. My great aunt on my dad's side committed suicide by gassing herself. I wish there was an open dialogue at that time. I remember going to their funerals and hearing relatives whispering about how the deceased were "feeling blue". Why didn't they help them? Now they're crying over their casket. My friends fought for me. They dragged me to the hospital.

Vanessa: Do you find that you push people away?

Tajsha: Yeah I've pushed people away. Their words of wisdom just weren't working. It makes the condition worse for me. They tell me I should be fighting. When they tell me that, the language with which it is delivered does more harm than good. I know I am the one that has to do the work. Another reason I tend to push people away is because of being sexually, physically, and mentally abused as a child.

Vanessa: Do you feel that your current state of mental illness is largely due to genetics or the abuse you suffered as a child?

Tajsha: Both. I get triggered when I go into certain rooms in my family's home. For example, I don't go into my grandmom's bathroom because that is where she told me as a young child that God does not love me because of the sins of my mom and dad. My mom and dad are first cousins. By that time, I had already been molested by a family member and this added to my depression.

My parent's bathroom is another place that triggers me because it was there that I was physically abused. Because I would get beat, it drove me towards perfectionism so I could avoid being abused. I learned to wear a mask early on. I never told my parents I was molested because I thought they would think it was my fault. They never acknowledged the signs: I stopped wanting to go outside, I wouldn't let my mom lotion my legs, etc.

Vanessa: Can you discuss your experience with how race may have exacerbated or contributed to symptoms of your condition?

Tajsha: I remember my white friends freely talking about seeing a therapist, meanwhile I hid my visits to the school counselor. There's a stigma against us being mentally ill. I had a white friend who explained to me how she was on Xanax for an anxiety disorder as if it were no big deal. I remember thinking how much her parent's must've loved her because they took the time to get her treated.

Vanessa: Are you on medication now?

Tajsha: No. I was cut off of Medicaid.

Vanessa: Lastly, what are some things that help you?

Tajsha: Taping into my Native American ancestry by going to the sweat lodge, practicing yoga and meditation.

MIND CHATTER
BY MISIA DENEA

I did not sign up for this
Put in psychotherapy at age 17
Prozac and Zoloft made me numb
Paxil made my heart jump into my throat

Depression is no stranger to me
The blues song states it well
"If it wasn't for you bad luck, I wouldn't have no luck at all..."
Well damn, what is a women to do with years of childhood incest, teenage
date rape?
Binge eat, mindless sex, suicidal tendencies...
I need to be numb... I need to escape
Why the fuck am I disgusted with the reflection in the mirror?

I did not sign up for this...
Ok can this evil game of tortured colored girl be over?
Why can't i just be thin, white and financially secure?
Isn't that the hallmark of happiness?
Get me out of here
I did not sign up for this
I'll time travel back to where I am really from
I know I am the Black Gold of the Sun
Ride the waves of the ocean
Help me Olokun

Remove the shackles
Let me dance on Mother Earth
to the beat of my own drum
take me back to when I held my head
High
Before the dawn of time
Before captivity
Take me back to when I was Free

Misia Denéa has a B.F.A in Dance from Temple University's Esther Boyer College of Music and Dance, and also graduated from The Institute for Integrative Nutrition and the Raw Food Institute. She is the owner/founder of Hatha Holistic Integrative Wellness. Her mission is to Coach, Heal, and Transform women who want to shift their relationship to themselves and cultivate holistic habits to feel sexy, vibrant, and liberated with yoga, meditation, and mindful eating. She has lead yoga trainings, dance workshops and retreats at yoga studios, Universities & Colleges, throughout the US and in the Caribbean/Latin America.

BLACK AND WHITE RABBITS
BY EV REHEARD

My mother is from South Korea. My father is an American of German and Irish decent.

For my entire life, I have watched people's faces as they meet me. More than half greet me with curiosity about my heritage. A few tell me they assumed I was simply white or an Asian girl with very light features or dyed hair.

I always dealt with being labeled as two things that never seemed to completely fit. The other half was always disagreeing. When I was 30, I was given another label that no one could identify clearly… a diagnosis: Borderline Personality Disorder (BPD).

Black and white thinking, literally.

My mental health, like my "color" is invisible.

People notice, but they do not understand what it means. I barely understand it. It took thirty years of confusion before enough voices explained to me how most people see from a different perspective, express themselves with different words… and some are not even expressing themselves at all. Some are simply going through pleasantries and courtesies, expecting I should read their minds.

Well, I have a doctor's note that says I am not supposed to read minds. I have read the books about my condition. I sift through the psychological studies and articles. The therapy prescribed for my condition, in both Eastern and Western medicine necessitates that I spend a great deal of time and energy being mindful to stay in the present moment. The here and now.

Here… and

Now.

Because until someone gave me this label, I wandered around daydreaming all day! I loved it. I never imagined life could be enjoyable lived out loud. I was too busy living in my head.

Life was just a book that I could never finish.

Problem was, I got writer's block and could not imagine my way out of the story where I had landed.

It took me almost two years, but now… Just now, things started to go way better than I could have ever imagined. I just let go.

This is still really scary to most of my family. I feel myself becoming defensive around them all of the time. When they talk to me, I feel disapproval- and I feel my confidence and motivation wane.

I play this out in my head. Am I just a reflection of what they see? Or am I really making things happen by seeing them and following that white rabbit down another hole, all over again?

That is what I did a couple years ago, and that time I ended up in a mental hospital.

That time, I could not see what could go wrong. This time, I know what I am afraid of… and I am not afraid of it anymore.

When you are a suicidal person, and most people are not, I hear. But when you are, you cannot imagine death being scary. The thought is a relief.

The great part is, after you accept you are already dying from the day you were born, being suicidal is simply sort of being impatient with the process. It is control freak behavior. At the end of the day, it should be the one thing completely in one's own hands.

However, after one survives an attempt… a new reality sets in- No, even this, I do not control.

Hypothesis failed. Back to the drawing board.

Well then, it is time to try something new… Many new somethings …and someones too, sometimes.

Two years of adjusting my mind. Two years of changing the thoughts that said, "Your skin, hair, and eyes should have been a different color. Your body should have been a different shape" to "You are so lucky. You have this lovely body."

It is now the only thing I hate about BPD. That I am still considered to have a "disorder", an "illness".

Now I know how to be self-aware and practice radical acceptance. Now I see that licensed therapists are hanging out at the same yoga classes, meditation groups, and Reiki schools that I am. Some of them even go to church. I am pretty sure most of them have a handle on this living thing just about as well as I do. We are taught to regulate our emotions and vent about them later. If we are wise, through an artistic medium.

Life is the food we eat. Art is… the shit.

It makes the flowers grow.

But the words "disorder" and "illness" make me think I should not trust my own opinion. Clearly, I do not think like everyone else, in a bad way. People seem concerned.

So… Do I keep following my disordered instincts? Or do I keep trying to fit this square peg in a round hole because it is what everybody else is doing?

My preliminary studies have shown that for me, following the crowd leads to suicidal thoughts and expensive hospitalizations. Following my heart has lead me to manifesting my dreams into reality.

Which rabbit would you follow?

INTERVIEW WITH NICHOLE WEBB

Vanessa: Nichole, thanks so much for agreeing to participate in this project. When were you diagnosed with mental illness?
Nichole: I was diagnosed with clinical depression in 2002, though I've had bouts of mania since then.

Vanessa: Do you have any co-occurring illnesses?
Nichole: Yes, hypertension and tachycardia.

Vanessa: Have you ever been hospitalized for mental illness?
Nichole: Yes. After high school, I attended community college. At around age nineteen or twenty, I began using drugs and alcohol. I was kicked out of my home and lived on the streets for a few days. A friend of mine found me a place to stay with people she knew and I lived there for a bit. While staying there, I began cutting. One time I cut too deep and my friend took me to the hospital. I was immediately admitted into their mental health unit and stayed there for a week and a half.

Vanessa: Have you ever had any suicide attempts?
Nichole: I've taken pills a few times.

Vanessa: Have you found your friends or family to be supportive?
Nichole: My dad and stepdad tried to be there for me but I wasn't fully honest with them about how bad things were. Through my talks with them, I found out that mental illness and substance abuse ran in my family. My mom's side of the family was not as supportive. Maybe it's a cultural thing, but we just didn't discuss mental health. I had a lot of support from my friends though.

Vanessa: Have you ever been medicated?
Nichole: I was prescribed Zoloft. I didn't respond well to it. It made me more suicidal and I also developed a tick. I felt disoriented. I was neither depressed nor anxious…I was just there. I discontinued Zoloft within a few months of leaving the mental hospital. I haven't tried any other medication.

Vanessa: Have you tried non-medicinal interventions?
Nichole: Yes! Art, playing and listening to music, drawing, abstract painting, yoga, and meditation all play a huge role in controlling my emotions. Yoga and meditation in particular helped me to get to know myself and recognize my cycles. With time, I've begun to notice when something is off and am able to give myself what I need.

Vanessa: How has your lifestyle affected your healing process?
Nichole: The stress of being a single mom makes it more challenging, but on the other hand my son motivates me. I can't afford to stay in bed for days on end when he needs to be cared for. He makes me want to push through my depressive episodes. I have a Bachelor's degree in Therapeutic Recreation and recently graduated from massage therapy school. I love my career. It gives me a sense of joy and wholeness. Considering we spend most of the hours of the day at work, it helps that I love what I do for a living!

MENTAL HEALTH
BY MR. NATE BUTLER

"If there was a real war on drugs, it would have to start in the psychiatric ward of the nearest crazy house, because what the Mad Scientist did to the mind of the so-called American Negro is some sick shit."

My name is Nate Butler; I have been incarcerated for 25 years now. I have been housed in several different state prisons fighting off the beast. The beast is something mental that every Black man knows about especially those of us trapped behind these prison walls.

Over the years, I've seen prison officials use tactics to break a prisoner who they deem as uncontrollable or violent.

I've seen strong stand-up dudes transformed into shivering, dribbling idiots, their minds turned into mush by psychotropic drugs on the mental health tip. A psychiatrist employed by the Department of Corrections is brought in to study a lot of prisoners and they usually diagnose you with some kind of mental illness. This takes me back to America's darkest moments when a mad doctor named Samuel Cartwright coined the term *Drapetomania*. He said: "In 1864 the desire for any enslaved African to be free, they must suffer from a form of psychosis."

Once the diagnosis is put down on you and the medication is ordered, if the prisoner refuses to take them they're thrown inside the R.H.U. (Restricted Housing Unit) and isolated completely until they comply.

These medications are highly addictive and the prisoner quickly becomes addicted to them. They make you eat a lot and sleep all day. The result is an overweight, slow walking, quivering, zoned out person. A prisoner who was once a warrior is transformed, now he is just a shell of himself.

Incredibly, some prisoners recover from this type of torture. Very few of them ever return 100% to their former self, some get back to 85% of their former self, still, that's some feat.

It should be noted that the law states in general no prisoner can be forced to take psychotropic drugs. However, in general, prison officials operate above and beyond the law with impunity. Not only do they do this but the vast majority of the times their actions are justified by the courts.

Presently, prisoners are denied access to the courts by exorbitant filing fees they can't afford. In addition, there are stringent convoluted rules most mental health prisoners are too under-educated to follow. Very rarely do the courts appoint counsel to assist prisoners in filing lawsuits or complaints.

The situation is such that less than 1% of all aggrieved mental health prisoners ever file a complaint to the courts and 99% of those are dismissed without a trial.

Not only are most mentally ill prisoners under-educated for the task of legally protecting their rights, prison officials frown upon and or deter others prisoners from assisting them. Back in 1996, our sick people loved the first 'Black' President, Bill Clinton. He passed legislations that have put so many barriers and pitfalls to deny prisoners' access to the courts, even trained lawyers have trouble navigating the process.

In the mid-1990s, politicians used the propaganda of 'frivolous lawsuits' to pass legislations that virtually deny prisoners access to the courts. It was political posturing, part of the anti-crime, anti-prisoner rights, right-wing agenda, put forward to appease the new manifestation of racism, that of judicial lynching.

"The pen is mightier than the sword."

When you venture into the realm of mental health, you must always go back go to the scene of the original crime- history! Empire understands war, and when you enter war, the mind of the people must be your target, because once the mind is slaughtered, the body becomes the property of the slayer. Imagine a mind with zero ideas a brain firing on zero cylinders. This was the struggle confronting so many of our leaders who had the heart to help out. Remember, we are still a sick people from the Ghost of Slavery, and dealing with the Black mind, if there is no intelligence, it has to be created, no perception of history, it has to be inserted, a corrective surgery has to be performed. With surgery, the pain of change, of transformation is post-operative. The mind of a mentally ill person is childlike and a child's mind learns less through analysis and more through example.

Most of us suffer from post-traumatic stress of having our minds ethnically cleansed.

Nathaniel Butler (KZ8135) is a writer, currently incarcerated in one of Pennsylvania's State Prisons.

PAIN: WHERE WE MEET FACE TO FACE
MR. NATE BUTLER

I look within these four prison walls, and I must find a way out. I have been locked within these walls for 24 years now, but I have not been alone. For pain is here with me. Day after day, week after week, month after month, and year after year.

I have felt the darkness of you, Pain, all around me, within these walls, waiting, looking with your eyes of fire and yet, you look upon me with a dark stare, darker than any night.

From the time of my beginning, from the day that I came forth into the light, the darkness of you, Pain, was upon me at that very moment. Oh how I see the beauty of you as you sit upon your high mountain with your sword of death in hand, and darkness itself is your beauty. Yes, I know what you look like and how you hunger in your wait for my mind and life.

Madness has tried to take hold of my mind, and I fear that it was you, Pain, that sent madness to try and take hold of me, for you have a strong desire to meet me face to face, and take my mind and my life now at this very moment. Surely you, oh Pain, can do better than sending madness, for madness shall never prevail against me.

I am not like the weak, heartless ones. For, they are the ones who will not fight for their lives or freedom any longer. They choose to not embrace the next sunrise, nor embrace the blue skies above, nor behold the stars that are twinkling so brightly in the dark heavens at night. They get beyond these prison walls that hold them by seeking their poison, a handful of pills, or self-lynching. The weak fools, they become yours before their true time in life has come to its glorious end.

Look deep within my soul, Pain, and you shall surely know that I am not one of the weak, heartless ones. I will continue in my daily struggle against you. I fear not the darkness of your face. I fear that we shall meet face to face here, inside this cage that's been holding me for the last 24 years.

To meet you face to face here and now would surely destroy part of the souls of those who love me so dearly. When it comes to having true understanding about human life, and what it means to love and be loved, you, oh dark one, the Department of Corrections, who sit upon your mountain of darkness, of pain. You are lost and dead to the full understanding of mankind's love of life.

For you are Pain, a seeker and taker of the loves of all who live. You were created from your beginning to be who you are, Pain, the dark one. I pray daily that the stars of heaven shall hold you within their bright light, or that the mighty winds take hold of you. For I need more time, more time to get beyond these four prison walls.

I know that I shall not prevail over you forever, for time is on your side, it is your strength over.

The day will surely come when you and I must meet face to face, oh you, dark one, please know that at the very moment of our meeting face to face, I shall smile at the beauty of your dark face, for I do see the beauty of your dark face, for I do see the beauty in life, as well as the beauty in your pain. For I am the product of the mean streets of Philadelphia, Pennsylvania, I shall not fall before my glorious and true end.

Nathaniel Butler (KZ8135) is a writer, currently incarcerated in one of Pennsylvania's State Prison.

THE MAMA THAT YELLED:
BLACK MOTHERING THROUGH DEPRESSION
IRESHA PICOT

She yelled all the time.
Yelled about the house not being cleaned.
Yelled about my school work.
Yelled about spending too much time on the phone.
Yelled that the music was too loud.
She just always yelled.
I can remember thinking about cutting her vocal box out of her once. Or a
few times. I told her this in a fit of rage, when I was about 16. She just
looked at me and yelled some more. I am pretty sure that Audre Lorde was
talking about my mama when she said, "I am deliberate and afraid of
nothing".
My mama didn't always yell. When I was a young girl, my mama was noted
for her laughter and the jokes she told to not only her own children, but to
the children who would come over to our home. They loved my mama's
jokes and her eagerness to make everyone laugh.
I have fond memories of my mamas as a child. She used to let me rest on
her lap all the time or ride me on the back of her bike as we went on
adventures through our small country town. As the youngest of three girls,
I used to have her all to myself when my sisters would go off to school and
my dad went to work. And we had fun. Going to her girlfriend's home, to
the beauty salon, out to eat; wherever my Mama went, I was right there with
her. Even when my sisters came home from school, there were good times

to be had by all. On Saturdays, she would walk the three of us, hand and hand to the Three Guys restaurant for pizza across the train tracks from our home; telling us jokes the whole way. On Sundays, we awoke to pancakes being cooked, and the Alvin and the Chipmunks record being played on our record player. We danced, and laughed. We enjoyed our Mama.

Then things changed. My dad became addicted to crack cocaine. Things became hard. My mother started to laugh less. She started yelling more. Her workload increased as well.

With my daddy's addiction, his paycheck would be depleted in two days. Sometimes the same day. Bills weren't getting paid and we struggled. We moved at least once a year. Sometimes twice. Our electric was never on. We couldn't even afford the $25 dollars for our books at school. My mother started working 2 to 3 jobs to compensate for my father's habit. She rarely slept, going from one job to the next. We hardly saw her and when we did, we stayed out of her way if we didn't want to be yelled at. Even moments that seem to be fun times with my mother turned sour. I can vividly remember on one of her rare off days, watching our favorite television show, *Martin*, together. We went from busting it up, laughing loudly at Martin's punch lines, to her becoming upset. Her mood could change liked a light switch, as if she would suddenly look up and realize that the house was dirty and the yelling and cursing would start. "Why is the house so fucking dirty?" or "I work all damn day and no one washed the dishes". It got to a point where we started to enjoy her being away from the home. It was peaceful.

She also developed these control issues. Probably because her own life was spinning out of control. She couldn't make our plight much better, even by working several jobs. She couldn't stop her husband from smoking crack. The only little bit of control she had was overpowering her children. If we didn't do something my mama wanted, she went into her rages, she hid the home telephone when she went to work, and we were trapped in the house without being able to communicate to anyone. She did this too with simple things such as the soap powder. If she was mad at us, we couldn't wash clothes. This was the same for the iron, the cable cord, the soda. She had to have control over everything. Over us. But not herself.

I have great empathy for my mama's plight now. She struggled to raise children in poverty by herself, and in return, she developed mental health problems. That does not negate the fact that as a young black girl, I became impacted by her actions. As a mental health professional, I now understand that my mother was suffering from stress related mental health issues. My mama was unhappy in her own life. Even with a husband present, she was raising her children up as an overworked, Single Black Mother. She fell into her own stereotypes. In Black communities, Black women aren't supposed to crack. We are not supposed to become depressed, even when we experience factors such as poverty, poor and unstable living conditions, psychosocial challenges, and white supremacy.

Just because we are Black and Woman.

Black Women, as the keepers of children, suffer silently. They have to be present under this harsh system to raise vibrant children. A difficult task at best, because if our children do not flourish under our rearing, it is the mamas who have to answer for those failures. As the great bell hooks stated, we must "cherish our mothers", not just uphold them for the things that they do for us, but also assist them in making their load lighter. If we see a mother struggling, we have to be there as a community to lift her up and when we see her not doing well, we have to be able to assist in creating a space for her to be able to say that she is tired and needs help. Yes, we need to cherish mothers.

After I wrote my piece, I decided to not only share the content with my mother, but to also include her voice. What follows is an interview that I did with her when she came to visit me on 5/14/15:

Iresha: What were some of the struggles you faced with basically raising your children by yourself?

Mom: Trying to pay the bills. The bills were always on my mind. It was a constant worry. Also, for five years, I did not work, and with your father's drug problem, not only was I thrown into having to go to work, I had to work 2 to 3 jobs, which means I always had to go to work and leave my children around.

Iresha: The name of this piece is called "The Mama that Yelled". Do you think that you yelled a lot when you were raising your children?

Mom: To be honest, yes. I didn't know that at the time, but I see how it affected you now. My mother yelled, and her mother yelled. We were just a yelling family and it seemed normal. But yes, I can say I yelled at you all a lot.

Iresha: Do you ever reflect back on that time and wonder what you could have done differently? If so, what are you doing now with your children to change those patterns?

Mom: I could have been a better mom with my attitude and did family things with my children.

Iresha: Do you think that you suffered from depression at that time?

Mom: Absolutely. I just had so much on me and it was kind of hard. I was away from my family in DC and so I had no family here in Virginia for my own personal support. Your dad's family helped me out a lot with raising you all, but I had no one to talk about my husband being on drugs and having to struggle. I cried all the time. I cried in the morning, at work. Especially, when your father would come home on pay day and there was no money. He had spent it on drugs.

Iresha: What advice would you give mamas, raising children by themselves?

Mom: Whatever you do, put your children first. Be a good mother to your children. And for the mothers and their own health, use your support systems and look to God; because to me that is looking up.

INTERVIEW WITH LYDIA KIRKLAND

Lydia Kirkland is a mother from southern New Jersey. In 2013, she lost her daughter, Brianna. As with many grieving parents, Lydia has been living with depression and post-traumatic stress disorder since her daughter's passing.

Vanessa: When did Brianna pass away? What was the cause?
Lydia: She passed away on Feb.24, 2013. She was misdiagnosed by the ER and passed from Type I diabetes. Her original diagnosis was a virus that was supposed to take its course and I was told she would be fine. The next morning I found she had passed away in her bedroom.

Vanessa: Tell us about Brianna and some of your favorite moments with her.
Lydia: I have so many memories of Brianna that I cherish. However, one of my favorite times to think of is Christmas time. She was my decorating partner. We would decorate the tree together, [hang] stockings with our names on them and listen to Christmas music dancing around the house. I also think about how smart she was and when she was young all the books we would read together.

Vanessa: How are you handling the grieving process? Have cultural, religious, or spiritual based traditions played a role?
Lydia: With the grieving process many say I am handling it well, I'm not sure what that means. I suppose to many people because I am able to get dressed and function on what they may think seems to be a "normal" level they say I am doing well. I struggle like many do, grief comes and goes like the ocean waves of emotions come in and go out. I remember after Brianna died, I said I felt like I buried a part of myself that day and I did, she was

literally a part of me for at least nine months. And she is forever a part of my story. I think with the death of a child you deal with guilt a lot. You struggle as a parent because this was a life you were to protect and help grow. With my child passing, I feel I wasn't able to do that. I wrestle with my emotions constantly because although I feel guilty I also know I cannot decide who lives and who dies. I have turned to God more than before and He is getting me through it. When you feel like you cannot relate to others because they simply have not experienced such a loss, I believe a lot of people reach within. I believe God lives within and so I turn there for peace. Even with a spiritual foundation, that doesn't mean we are automatically better. We still exist in this realm and the reality is my daughter is not here. However, understanding Jesus and who He is and His love, I have hope I will see Brianna again and that helps with my grief.

Vanessa: Are you seeing a mental health professional? If so, are they treating you for a specific condition (i.e. depression, PTSD, etc.)?
Lydia: I do see a therapist and have been since 2013. I am being treated for depression, anxiety and PTSD by my therapist and family doctor.

Vanessa: Do you have a solid support system (including, but not limited to: therapists, psychiatrists, friends, family, support groups, colleagues, etc.)? If so, in what ways do they support you?
Lydia: I have some support with family and friends as they participate sometimes with memorials or different events I have, when Brianna's birthday comes around or during the anniversary of her death. I have also gone to a support group for parents that have suffered the loss of a child called The Compassionate Friends. This group talks about their grief and their children, it helps to be able to relate to those who know your pain.

Vanessa: What kinds of things do you do for self-care?
Lydia: I read books on personal growth, have done yoga, pray and read my Bible. I have also returned to school to obtain my Masters. I try to take care of myself mentally and believe these things have helped me.

Vanessa: Tell us about the organization you started in your daughter's name.
Lydia: I started a foundation in memory of my daughter called Filling Buckets for Brianna. Brianna was 13 when she passed away; after she died I was able to get her notebooks from school. In one of her notebooks I found a poem she wrote about filling buckets. This poem talked about people being empty and how we should fill their buckets (lives). I took this poem and made it the central theme of the foundation. Our organization raises money to help parents that have suffered the loss of a child from

birth to 18 years of age with funeral and headstone cost. Right now we are only working with a local funeral home, in the future I look forward to doing more. Part of our mission is to help fill the lives of others by giving of ourselves. We can be found on Facebook and have a website www.fillingbucketsforbrianna.com, if you would like to learn more about our organization or donate. I believe by sharing yourself with someone else you can bring healing to others as well as receive healing for yourself.

Lydia Kirkland currently lives in Pine Hill, NJ. She has a Bachelors in Psychology from Rutgers University and is currently working toward her Masters in Admin. of Human Services at Wilmington University. She has been working in the human service field for 19 years. She is the founder of Filling Buckets for Brianna; a NJ Nonprofit Corporation. She is also a single mother and believes that is her most important job.

SLEEPING BEAUTY
BY NATASHA C. DAVIS

Natasha was diagnosed with learning disabilities when she was 3 years old. She has had difficulties with struggling with depression and narcolepsy. As a teenager, she was diagnosed with Aspergers (Autism).

(REGARDING MY NARCOLEPSY)

Sleep, sleep, sleep
  Day in and day out.
Stay asleep, keep sleeping
  Through the quiet and the loud.
Wake up sleeping beauty,
  Wake up, wake up, wake up.
Why won't she wake?
  Can she? Does she even hear me?
Sleeping Beauty can't wake up…
  Not because she won't.
Sleeping beauty sleeps
  Because she can't control her sleeping spells.
She's been under this sleeping spell
  Since she was born.
Can't control it,

Or break the spell.
Then one day, comes some news....
    A cure that could help Sleeping Beauty out.
To live life as fairly normal as she can,
    She has to start using certain medication.
Now sleeping beauty can live her life,
    She can function quite well, and controls her sleeping spells.
Things that people said Sleeping Beauty couldn't do,
    Now that she's in control, is no longer the truth!
She can still drive, learning as she goes,
    She is able to stay awake.
Knowing she can do anything she dreams,
    And deal with life's highs and lows.

WATCH ME
BY NATASHA C. DAVIS

I'm always told I can't do this…
So don't bother, don't try…

I'm told countless times to stop dreaming,
I won't make it at all.

I dream of becoming a dancer/choreographer and living in New York.
I dream of writing "best seller" books, acting and more.

Stop living in fantasy land and come back to reality…
With the way your mind works, I think you're losing your sanity.

I may be slow to learn and understand….
But don't think you can tell me what I can and cannot do….if I say I
can.

So go ahead keep telling me no, it'll make this even sweeter when I do.
"You can't, you can't (never!)" Two words; WATCH ME!

The things I wanna do,
The places I wanna go, and the people I wanna meet…

It's exciting to me,
Knowing that I'm getting there....

That I'm pushing to make it happen,
To go all the way....
Some things are difficult,
And might be hard to pull off...

But I won't quit, I won't give in!
I'm very patient, stubborn and determined.

I want this, to make my dreams come true;
I'm gonna fight for it, and I believe in miracles!

I may be slow to learn and understand,
But don't think you can tell me what I can or cannot do...if I say I can.

So go ahead, keep telling me NO,
It'll make this even sweeter when I do!

"You can't, you can't (never!)"
Two words; WATCH ME!

I'm definitely the biggest dreamer in my family
To me, it's either dream big, or don't at all!

I've known what I want to do,
And what I want to be since infancy

I've been working hard,
And striving towards my goals in life

If at the end of this road,
I'll be living in the spotlight...
I may be slow to learn and understand,
But don't think you can tell me what I can or cannot do....if I say I can.

So go ahead, Keep telling me NO!
It'll make things sweeter when I do!

"You can't, You can't (Never!)"
Two words; WATCH ME!

WHAT'S IT LIKE?
BY NATASHA C. DAVIS

What's it like to live with learning disabilities?
To know that the basics like Math and Science are your enemies?

What's it like to go to school…
To know you can't keep up, making you feel like a fool?

What's it like to get a job?
To learn the rules and play the game?

But at the end,
You get the blame?

A history of users and fakes….What's it like to give it your all,
If at the end, all they do is take?

What's it like to wish away the madness?
To wish you could do more to think differently?

What's it like when you're mentally challenged?
Your memories jacked, and your past memories absent?

What's it like to do daily tasks?
To try to get an order right, only to remember it wrong?

What's it like to know you didn't see it coming when everyone tells you,
But you didn't get it then?
What's it like to not understand how to socialize?
And when you're being laughed at instead?

What's it like when you can't tell the difference between a lie and the
truth?
When people say one thing, only to make up an excuse?

What's it like to have half your common sense?
To know some things naturally, while waiting to learn the rest?

What's it like to have family
Who loves and cares to keep you going and succeed in life?

I know what it's like,
How it feels to be me....

Thankfully I have a mother who fights,
And she'll never quit, and she's my everything!

A COMPLICATED NORMAL
BY VANESSA HAZZARD

I thought I was well. It's been over a year since I stopped cutting and almost two years since I've been released from the hospital after being treated for borderline personality disorder, bipolar disorder and PTSD. Since then, I've held a steady job and re-enrolled in a Bachelors degree program. My life had been successfully recalibrated after years of trauma. That life was so far in the rear view mirror, so small, that it seemed just a blip on the radar compared to all the good things that lay before me.

I felt normal for the first time in my life. Not bland normal, just sane normal; a stable, healthy, functional normal. I should've known that my kind of normal is a bit more complicated when a seemingly innocent hug from behind triggered a rush of memories long forgotten. It wasn't even so much the memories themselves that bothered me. It was the feelings of being dirty, used-up, and insignificant that accompanied them. I'm not lazy when it comes to my mental health. I do the work, as tiresome as it may be, and yet this occurrence sent me into a tailspin. How can some people shake off their woes, while others, like myself, are just left shaken?

That night, I tried to sleep it off, but to no avail. Through all the tossing and turning and tears, I couldn't escape myself. I remembered that I had an expired bottle of Valium with a few pills left inside. Hoping they still had some potency; I washed down a pill with a sip of cheap wine and waited for my mind to settle but it wasn't long before the psychosis began. This trance-like reality was a familiar place for me, just a few years prior when the symptoms of PTSD were at its peak. I was slow and heavy, yet deliberate when I grabbed the razor in my drawer and did as I've done many times before. I cranked up the classical music station I was listening to and began slicing my inner thighs. The razor slid across my skin like a bow on violin strings. I always want to be a violin when I'm in this state. It's so beautiful, fine and delicate, attributes I always fell short of embodying.

At first, my slicing was a bit haphazard, a few cuts here and there. I just wanted to see my blood escape from the inside of my body. Then, as the music grew louder, I became increasingly more intentional with the cutting, as my need to be a violin intensified. I was focused and on a mission. By this point, my mind was completely fragmented yet a small part of me knew I was obsessed with an impossibility. But the orchestral violins, like a pied piper, led my other parts further and further away from the stable, healthy, functional normal that I worked so hard to achieve. I began cutting a musical staff in my leg. Then I sliced another. Then one more. I kept going until the violins released their hold and I was *re-minded*. I'm not sure how much time went by, but when I looked down, I had cuts that spanned the length of both my inner thighs. The drops of blood dripped out like notes in a fucked up lullaby, as it was successful at putting me to sleep.

The days and nights that followed were more of the same. I'd put on a happy, pleasant face at work. I'd help my son with his homework, make dinner, and then head upstairs to cut while he was playing with his uncles. I was good at faking normalcy when all the while I was slipping deeper and deeper into depression. Truth is, I was battling a depressive episode for a few weeks, but was able to keep it at bay. Between medication, meditation, and working out, I knew I was able to work through it as I have done in the past. This trigger though…it snuck up on me and pulled me under. For days, I was a melancholy mass of flesh and shame drudging through what felt like molasses towards the *mights* at the end of the tunnel. I *might* be healthy one day. I *might* be successful. I *might* never have to take medication again. The thought of my son was like dangling a carrot in front of me to keep me running towards those *mights*, instead of succumbing to my current reality…my inner thighs were full of fresh, self-inflicted scars… the results of a poor and dangerous coping mechanism. One that I sadly and shamefully enjoyed.

When bedtime came, my son came upstairs crying for his dad. His dad and I have been divorced and living in separate households for a few years now. Even when I think that my son has processed our separation and accepted that he'll see his dad only on weekends, by mid-week he usually begins to cry for him. I do as I always do. I put him on my lap and rock and embrace him. The weight of his, lanky, seven-year-old body stings my scars and I am immediately filled with hypocrisy. How can I console him when I can't healthily attend to my own depression?

After his tears subside, he asks me to read him a book, *Something Beautiful* by Sharon Dennis Wyeth. The little girl in the book is in search of something beautiful in her neighborhood and questions her neighbors on what they think is beautiful. In the end, the girl's mother says that she is her something beautiful. I looked at my son and said, "…and you're my something beautiful". Without hesitation, he replied, "…and you are mine, mommy". I couldn't help but burst into tears while my son drifted off to sleep. This tainted, scarred body and complicated mind was his mommy…and he thought her beautiful. That was his normal and I hope that one day it becomes my own.

NOT READY TO DIE BUT WANTING TO DIE: DEPRESSION, HIP HOP AND THE DEATH OF CHRIS LIGHTY
BY ROSA CLEMENTE

"We need a very serious and healing discussion on depression for the Hip Hop generation. As one who suffers from depression myself, it breaks my heart to see those lose this very difficult and often lonely battle." 8/30/12 - My Facebook status after hearing of Chris Lighty's death

Right now I should be finishing a paper for my independent study. But I just heard the news about Chris Lighty's death. Though I never meet him, being part of the Hip Hop village, I always heard good things about him. Reading my sister, Joan Morgan's, one word post on Facebook, "devastated", I broke down and thought, another possible suicide in our village. Why is this happening? All of us living and breathing are dealing with a myriad of challenges, especially financial ones, so what is it that makes one want to kill themselves? And why is there so much silence in communities of color? We all grew up hearing about suicides, and for a long time I believed that only white kids killed themselves. When I was in high school, there was a rash of suicides that I heard about, read about. I would say to my friends, "white kids are crazy". Little did I know that I myself might have been a little bit "crazy".

It was not until 2005 that I was diagnosed with bipolar disorder and depression. It wasn't until I was 34 and after a very hard pregnancy, in which I suffered from a rare disease, hyper-emesis, along with postpartum depression, that I finally admitted to myself that I had been suffering with depression since my mid-twenties and I desperately needed help.

Depression manifests itself in many ways. For me, it manifested as manic episodes of high energy, no sleep, compulsive cleaning and bursts of anger. As I look back at my life, I recall encounters in which I acted irrationally, impulsively and destructively, sometimes publicly. I recall episodes of manic states in which I would stay up for days, clean and write like a fiend. When the panic state ended I would shut down and isolate myself for days in my room and cry myself to sleep, thinking of death.

In the subsequent seven years since my diagnosis I have sought treatment that includes medications, talk therapy, acupuncture and more holistic techniques. I have great days and some very dark ones, but I believe I am better and as I continue to live, I have come to truly understand this disease. One of the hardest things was telling friends who would then tell me all the evils of these meds and urge me to drink this tea, do this exercise, eat this food or just go out and take a walk, it's just the blues. As well-meaning as my friends were they just did not get it. Too many times those of us who deal with issues of mental health are silenced, ignored or told, "Everything will be all right", "You're strong" and often we want to scream back at them and say, "How do you know everything will be all right? I am sick of being strong!"

When we hear that it makes us shut down even more and retreat into that corner. When we see that look in your eye, we wish we never would have told you. No matter how many friends you have, how many people tell you they love you, these things do not cure depression. Some of us need medications, some of us cannot meditate or exercise our way out of it. Most of us inherited this and because of the silence in our families we may never truly know the extent to which this is passed down. I worry every day that my daughter has inherited this from me. Every time she cries, or shows signs of anxiety or stress, I am terrified that my little girl has "the gene."

I turned 40 this year, and I told myself I would live my life in my truth. Every day I wake up and I know that as much as I want to have a great day, the slip back into a depressive state lurks around the corner. Unfortunately, so many do not have the information, the networks or the support systems I do. Damn, so many are not privileged enough to have health insurance that covers mental health services. In one of my recent sessions with my therapist, she reminded me that there is no cure for depression, there is living with depression. Hip Hop and the larger community of Black and Brown, progressive, radical, and social justice activists must figure out a way to begin a dialogue, to not just break the silence around depression, but to stop the shaming of those who suffer this disease. Often times I feel that if I had an ailment that was physical or one that people could actually see, that their hearts and minds would be more open to that disability then to my mental health disability.

Today my silence stops. My shame ends. I am going to say the one thing you are never ever ever supposed to say; I wanted to die. Some of us reach this point, and it is the most frightening thing to say and feel. That day in April 2005, living in Brooklyn, I felt that feeling. The sick nauseating, head spinning, heart pounding feeling of wanting to die, visualizing how I would die and who would find me. As I lay on my bedroom floor ravaged with pain and tears, hoping to get the strength to walk to the 7 on Parkside and Prospect all I could feel is that soon this would be over, this monster inside of me would finally be gone and so would I. At that moment, a bit of light broke through and I did the one thing so many cannot and do not do, I picked up the phone. I called my best friend who called my mother who called my aunt who called a friend who is a psychiatrist. She stayed on the phone with me until my husband came home from work and the next morning I was in a doctor's office. Since that dark day in Brooklyn and until the day I am SUPPOSED to leave this world, I will be living with and battling this disease.

As I said, I never met Chris Lighty, but I keep imagining the moment he put that gun to his head, the pain and despair he must have felt is unfathomable. The thought of it makes me physically ill. As many write about his death, some will say he did not commit suicide, some will say that he showed no signs that he was depressed; some will blame his financial issues, some will be angry; some will ask themselves what they could have done, and unfortunately, some will pass judgment and some will never be able to admit that he lost his fight. The despair he must have been in might not have been noticeable even to those closest to him. Maybe no one knew. That's the thing about depression; it's a disease that is often suffered in silence, alone, behind a closed door, in the corner of a dark closet, under the covers of a bed.

I have often said that Hip Hop saved my life; now we need Hip Hop to do what it does best; tell the hard truth, bring people together to create the means to battle whatever ails us and try to save lives. For those of us in this

Hip Hop village suffering from this wretched debilitating disease we must break the silence, we must stop the shame. We must do it for those that are still living and in remembrance of those like Chris who did all they could to survive but lost their battle to this demon.

MY STORY
BY KHALIL BENNETT

My experience with the Department of Corrections educational/vocational system when I first was sent upstate appeared to be very beneficial. However, being young and rebellious; I didn't take advantage of it. This was in 1999. It took several years for me to awaken and mature a bit in 2003 before I would enter school with a little motivation from a few elders to try and get my GED; since I had an 8th grade education with the last grade attended being the 9th grade. The teacher assigned to assist me was one in a million. He was extremely open to new ideas, suggestions, and basically being taught himself, which actually makes a great teacher. So even though I did not achieve the goal (GED) I surely learned a lot from this teacher. After several years spent in different control units which impeded my ability to get my GED or any education prescribed by the administration upon release, here at Houtzdale, I was placed on a waiting list. Ridiculously, it took me over two years to attend school because the 'new' policy stated that those with minimums are on a first-come first-served basis. I ended up failing the GED twice because of the math. Since people were behind me on the waiting list, the staff made it their duty to give me the boot out. So I wisely took a trade in a business class. I was placed in a teacher's class who taught outside of the status quo and they eventually fired her. This was a year and a half ago. So hopefully, in the next couple of months, a new teacher will replace her and I can continue my business vocational class until I can enroll in the new diploma credit classes.

Every skill I've learned, all of the wisdom I have comes from self or other prisoners teaching me. And the rest comes from experience, observation, or reading. The greatest skill I taught myself is simple survival commonly known as self-preservation.

The day I was awakened and grew into self-knowledge and worldly affairs, I urgently dedicated myself to the struggle. So if I return to society, I will be entrenched in the changing of people's bad conditions. I believe that this is going to be a difficult task to do at times, yet I know that no conditions can last forever!

Because of my incarceration, my family, friends, and community, have taken dramatic changes words cannot describe. Some for the good and some for the bad, such as the loss of physical, spiritual, and mental life. Love has diminished. But most importantly, the understanding of the prisoner's life has been the hardest.

I haven't seen any changes being made for the good for those that resist against bad. The good I have seen is one becoming conscious to his surroundings and the world overall. The changes I would like to see is more resistance.

The only thing I believe will make our society better is when people finally get fed-up and decide no more will they simply accept the hardcore oppression of the government. I'm a revolutionary I believe in complete change!

What people in the public need to know about prison is that our enemies who built these death camps have utterly made prisons in the U.S. and abroad fair seeming. Basically places where human beings won't mind living!

While incarcerated, I went through a world/self-analysis very similar to Malcolm X, Kody "Monster" Scott, and Stanley "Tooki" Williams though the process of reading, writing, observing, but most importantly from extremely influential mentors from strong movements that fought got freedom. Due to my transformation; I suffered numerous physical, mental and spiritual attacks by facility staff members if the Department of Corrections. Subsequently, I have been in several control units (segregated units) around the state spending over 12 years in isolation units altogether. I am now a devoted and dedicated member/minister of the Nation of Islam. I organize prisoners regularly, give lectures, and hold legal seminars from time to time, author of a group pamphlets, and last but not least the founder of "Bulletin Response Squad" newsletter.

To contact Bro Khalil:
Khalil Bennett #DX-9353
P.O. Box 1000
Houtzdale, PA 16698

STRIPPED
BY PIERRE PINSON

One by one men are siphoned into a pallid room. There are two prison guards waiting intently. One busies himself with his paperwork, the other dons a despotic mask, his own necessity, a defense mechanism.
"Strip". It is an order, a foreign language to criminals, gangsters, and the underbelly of our society.
The prisoner obeys, an acquiesce, given the circumstance.
"The underwear too," instructs the guard. His bottom lip is wrapped around a wad of chewing tobacco. His breath is putrid. His glare is a challenge to the young, black prisoner…an exercise of power.
The prisoner concedes. Naked as a slave on the auctioneer's block, he is forced to follow the guard's instructions:

OPEN YOUR MOUTH. MOVE YOUR TONGUE. UP. DOWN. SIDE. OTHER SIDE. PULL YOUR EARS DOWN. LET ME SEE. LEFT EAR. RIGHT EAR. RUN YOUR HANDS THROUGH YOUR HAIR. LIFT YOUR HANDS TO THE CEILING AND LET ME SEE YOUR ARMPITS. HANDS IN FRONT. PALMS. BACK OF THE HANDS. LIFT YOUR PENIS. LIFT YOUR TESTICLES. TURN AROUND. LIFT YOUR RIGHT FOOT. WIGGLE YOUR TOES. LIFT YOUR LEFT FOOT. WIGGLE YOUR TOES. BEND OVER. SPREAD 'EM. COUGH.

The sadistic dance is done. A rite? A ritual. Violated, dismissed, confused, essentially a victim of a molestation that required no hands, only eyes. What does a man feel after this first impression, when this can be done at the whim of his overseers? He feels nothing.
Desensitization is the first symptom of a man suffering dehumanization.

Dehumanization is the primary instrument utilized in the psychological warfare of prison. Men are stripped, literally and figuratively, with deliberate intent. God-given names are replaced with numbers to ensure the "system" keeps track of its chattel. All elements of individuality are thwarted with rules and regulations to guarantee conformity. Clothing is replaced with garments issued by the administration. Hair "styles" are forbidden. With physical evidence of the man removed, he is left clinging to memories of who he was, and in many cases, what he could have been.

Prison is a monotonous assembly line of redundancy. Many men lose their minds in the complacency that routine creates. Like a child that is carried far into its years, some prisoners forget what it is to walk on their own volition. Soon, those that forget lose the desire to be ambulatory at all, hence institutionalization. The slave finds comfort in being relieved of problems assigned to the master. Those who grow or evolve in such sociological decrepitude, do so with diligence and a supreme enlightenment. It is a commonly held belief among prisoners that one plateaus at the age that he was incarcerated. It is against the odds of this stealth psychological warfare that despite being restricted by prison walls, men with self –taught discipline, purpose, and rebellion remain functioning human beings.

Some prisoners are never able to see the war being waged upon them. They are blind. Incessant barrages of Pavlovian tactics are poured into the prisoner's subconscious mind; numerous count bells that require the prisoner to stand and be accounted for. Bells that signal chow lines, bells that signal recreation, bells that signal passes, bells that signal superiority. These bells effortlessly move herds of men through the agonizing monotony. Even the walking dead are compelled to move by sheer habit. Men and boy alike fight this war willingly, unwittingly, many who were never considered men until they were charged with a crime. Most who were never viewed as equals of their white counterparts until they were forced to choose a jury of their "peers. In proliferation, black youth are marched in front of judges appointed by a system that has no regard for their futures or the composition of their communities. These men survive anticipating a freedom under the thumb of the "system", others are reduced to clinging to slivers of hope. Hope that hopelessly dangles in the hands of judges, small embers of hope that men within the system recognize their fellow man's humanity.

Stripped of his humanity, the prisoner is deemed useless by society. He is like a vampire, a being with human characteristics, but rarely recognized as human by his fellow man. Though he may have served his time, paid his debt to society, he cannot vote. If on parole, he cannot leave his state without permission, let alone leave the country. Employment opportunities are sure to keep him at or below poverty level. That is the future of the incarcerated…a freedom-less freedom. Facing these futures, many attempt to corral faith they never had or were unable to grasp. Seeking that which is greater than man to justify their suffering and in it, their existence. Religion becomes the foothold of the fallen. With minds unable to understand the deterioration of their humanity, only faith has the answers that logic has failed to supply.

In his state of dilapidation, man's primal instinct of self-preservation pushes him to survival. He will strive to heal his broken state by any means. With no concern or effort on the part of his captors, the prisoner finds a blessing; the greatest educations he many not have learned otherwise. Self-education, the education given by self and of self. Self-taught and self-produced forms of psychotherapy and/or spiritual redemption aid in this effort. Boldly, the prisoner throws himself on the table and performs open-heart surgery to mend his brokenness. A surgery performed by his own cumbrous hand, ill-equipped but diligently, the prisoner traverses a redoubtable terrain; a terrain within...a place inside of him. Through all he has endured, a prisoner should be able to face himself, recognize himself, understand himself, and most of all love himself. The prisoner will always emerge victorious, able to save himself in the throes of psychological warfare.

Pierre Pierson is a native from Pittsburg, PA. He is a writer and is currently working on several poetry books with the group Living On Vital Emotion Writers Group at SCI-Fayette.

Pierre can be contact at:
Pierre Pinson #EK2844
P.O. Box 999
50 Overlook Drive
LaBelle, PA 15450

US
BY ANONYMOUS

Black people have a secret sitting in their living rooms, lurking in their closets, and tucked away in that special room. We won't talk about it, would never publicize it and barely ask for help.

It's our brains. And like every other race on this planet, ours get sick too. I have worked in Special Education for a number of years now and I've seen it there. I've seen it in close family and friends. And if I'd ever give therapy more than a one session chance, I'm sure that I would have been diagnosed with some form of depression and or anxiety.

So why didn't I? Same reason we all don't. Because we are minorities and have been dealing with hardship eons and eons. Don't nobody need no shrink to deal. Just pray and push forward, like we've always done. That's who we are and that's what we do.

Sounds good, but this thinking has kept us handicapped from getting help for so long. Yes, we are strong. We have endured a whole lot more than other races. We have travailed. But we're still human! And we suffer the same as anyone else. So we need to start allowing ourselves to say that we're sick, and look for answers to our relief, just like anyone else. I have encountered a person, or 30 who has a story to tell about mental illness, but can't, because they---we, are bound by the race and the beliefs we carry of making such a declaration.

We have stories that we need to tell, healing that needs to begin. Here is mine.

I first felt it when I met my then boyfriend's brother. I mean, my boyfriend was crazy in many senses of the word, but his brother had a different air of strange about him. He wasn't quite with us. And I felt it even more when his mother cried on the phone the day that he went missing. It reached a fevered pitch the day I drove my boyfriend to see him. Seeing him strapped to a bed like something out of a thriller fucked with me for months.

Then I felt it again when I had become so knee deep in Special Education that I had almost become numb to it. I didn't think that there was anything that could jolt me out of my malaise. They were over there, and I was assisting them. Until I met him. Slim, intelligent young man who was often engaging with someone that no one else could see. All of my students had issues, so to speak. But during parent/teacher night, it was his father's anguish and attempt to diminish the obvious signs that I related to the most. I took him to my dreams and worry about him still, years after having left the school.

Finally, I felt it in the family of a Salone born girl. Up the street from me. Our families so close, I called her my sister. I knew there was something not right about her brother. Once someone I could at least hold a conversation with and laugh with, he had become so far gone that he'd only sit in front of his laptop or TV all day. Muttering to himself. Grunting hellos. I understood why having known me for so many years, how difficult it must have been to finally say his illness out loud.

In all my years working with the Special Needs population, why had these individuals touched me so? What did they all have in common? Guyana. Columbia. Sierra Leone. Respectively. They were no longer over there, stereotypical homeless people on the street, or white people. They are me. From the diaspora. Us. The us that don't get such diseases. Oh, I how I felt them.

What we are going through goes beyond shame. It is to the point where culturally, it really doesn't exist. Hell, I couldn't tell you the Temne or Krio word for schizophrenia or bipolar disorder. We come from cultures where the idea of mental illness is new, if it even exists at all. And if it does, it is still often described in terms of spiritual possession. Who do we tell? How do we get help? Is there help? What if someone found out? Oh, it is a shame felt in the spirit. So while the average person takes baby steps toward getting help, we will take ant steps.

I keep meeting us. Every day. And while the disease itself is not to be celebrated, the fact that we are seeking help should be. In spite of our deep-seated cultural fears.

INTERVIEW WITH SHANDA MICKENS
BY VANESSA HAZZARD

Shanda is a massage therapist born and raised in Philadelphia. She's a graduate of Roxborough High School and the National Massage Therapy Institute. She's a lover of love, life and the pursuit of the perfect order of buffalo wings. She's an avid music and movie lover, and enjoys spending time with her 4-year-old daughter Kyra Rose. Shanda also lives with bipolar disorder.

Vanessa: When were you diagnosed with bipolar disorder? What sorts of treatments have you received and were they successful?

Shanda: I was diagnosed with bipolar disorder at the age of 13. I was already in therapy for ADD. The doctors tried many combinations of medications. At one point, I was on Prozac, Lithium, and sleeping pills to balance out the Lithium. Sadly, they were not successful and actually had an adverse effect on me. Because of the effect that I've had from medications, I've been leery about taking prescription drugs and have been seeking other alternatives to manage my disorder.

Vanessa: What has it been like dating and parenting while living with mental illness?

Shanda: Dating and parenting while living with mental illness has been a struggle for me, but I'm constantly learning how to overcome the struggle and find a happy balance. I just learned to take things as they come and just live life one day at a time.

Vanessa: Do you have a support system of friends/family?
Shanda: I have a very strong support system of family and friends. One person who's the strongest person in my support system is my grandmother. She's my voice of reason and the only person that can snap me out of my depressed state.

Vanessa: Has bipolar disorder affected your career?
Shanda: Thankfully, my disorder has not hindered my career as a massage therapist.

Vanessa: Are other members of your family living with bipolar disorder?
Shanda: As far as I know, I'm the only member who is diagnosed with bipolar disorder.

ME
BY MARIE KANU

I've always felt it. The feeling of I Can't. It crept on me in my wide-eye, fantasy days of my youth. It was often at war with the feeling that there was nothing that I couldn't do. But often, I Can't won. I Can't also found an ally in an unexplainable, deep rooted sadness that I often felt. It surfaced in little ways at first. Sensitivity to the way the other children often ostracized me for my differences. Feeling that my mother did not really like me, much less love me. Feeling that I was doing something to make God angry (a product of being over-churched). The list of things that brought me down where many, and they seemed to be growing.

As I got older, I felt that there were times that the sadness would suffocate me. It seemed that my mind would create new and creative things for me to feel inadequate about. I didn't like my hair. Why was I so tall and gangly? Why was I so weird looking? Why did my glasses have to be so big? You shouldn't try out for the basketball team, you won't make it. Why are you still writing, it's a waste of time? No guy, will ever want you. You are not cute, at all! It was the kind of daily self-degradation that kept my head hanging low and made me feel tremendously anxious whenever entering a new social situation.

I was a mess. I would cry all the time for no one particular reason at all.

Just that I always felt worthless and useless and was exhausted from all of this inexplicable sadness. I wanted to do things besides be sad. But being sad became like my part-time job and I, at times, I had to will myself out of bed. I realized that I was getting deeper. I rarely socialized, and I Can't usually talked me out of trying out any extracurricular activities. I sat every morning in the hallway like a bump on a log waiting for my teacher to come to open the door. A boy inspired, or annoyed by my ennui decided to attempt to provoke me. He started with a little kick. I did nothing. He started with a bigger kick. I did nothing. Then he literally stood on top of my ankles and bounced! I. Did. Nothing. My grades were also that of a log's. Yet I was a terror at home. Lashing out at my parents over the smallest things.

It hasn't gotten much better since I've gotten older. Still feeling that I Can't and the stakes being higher. Not getting a proper job. Not getting my own place. Not writing. Not singing. Not dating. Not being able to pay my bills and feeling great anxiety about all of these things. I finally relented and sought some therapeutic assistance, then decided not to go back. Why? Because I can't go there long enough to be diagnosed with some form of crazy. That wouldn't be acceptable at all. Shit I'm black. And besides black, I'm African. I shouldn't need help to just live should I? I mean, that's just unacceptable. And as much as I've learned, as many mental illness cases I've encountered, I am still trying to get the woman in the mirror to seek help.

LOVE LETTER TO MOM
BY DEBRA POWELL-WRIGHT

1963: I was nine years old when my mother, Corrine Brown Powell, was hospitalized for nine months at Bellevue State Hospital in Pennsylvania, after having been diagnosed with schizophrenia. I couldn't visit her in the place that performed lobotomies, couldn't tell anyone because I didn't know anyone who had a sometimes crazy mother who had to take Lithium, or Haldol, or Thorazine, or Mellaril. In August 2001, I was forty-four when mom was diagnosed with cancer of the duodenum. She died that October. Six years later, I wrote her this love letter.

Hey Mom,

I'm reminiscing. Remember the little purple construction paper card that you gave me? The one with the little stars and hearts that you made at the day center?

You wrote on the card, "Thinking of you for always thinking of me, Debbie."

It's the prettiest card that I've ever gotten, and the one that means the most to me. No birthday card or Kwanzaa greeting can top that card that you left so benignly on my bed. Seriously; I still have it.

Remember how I used to do your hair—when you let me? Five huge braids that met at the center of your head and then circled into a bun. You looked like an African queen. Yaa Asantewaa. Nzingha. Amina of Zaria.

And with the outfit I bought for you to wear to your youngest daughter's wedding—the charcoal gray tunic, matching pants and head-wrap with the Ghanaian masks punctuating the silky cotton—you reminded me of Nefertiti. Her name means "the beauty that has come." You were really beautiful that day. Everybody said so.

All of our friends had only seen you with your worn out jeans and a drab over-sized sweater, sitting on our porch in 90-degree heat, talking to yourself, and chain-smoking cigarettes because I wouldn't allow you to smoke in the house. You almost burned it down; or as you said, it was one of the others in your head who hated the house—she's the one who liked fire.

Remember when you slipped on the ice and broke your wrist? Your two younger daughters could not stand to see the two metal pins stuck in your arm, knowing that the pus oozing from each eraser-sized hole would have to be cleaned on a daily basis. I could barely stomach it myself, but the wound had to be cleaned, and in fact, so did you. That was the first time that I had seen your bare breasts, your butt, your grown womanly-ness covered in mixed-gray hair. The bath became our mother-daughter ritual.

A few months later, you gave me the purple card.

I remember watching you day after day, at the kitchen table, drinking cup after cup of coffee, frantically scribbling when you thought that I wasn't watching. I could always see when a thought would come across your mind. You'd often mumble something under your breath, and then you'd start writing. Even though you probably were the only one who could decipher what the words meant—not that they weren't written in English—I could feel that they had some hidden powerful meaning, like hieroglyphics.

Remember how we loved to watch the shows with the Black characters—people who looked like us? *Julia, Sanford & Son, The Jeffersons, The Cosby Show*. And when I started listening to reggae music, you seemed to sense my intrigue with places far from Philadelphia. I recall one day in particular when I was sweeping the dining room, and you got up from your usual spot in the kitchen, maybe to go watch one of those TV shows. I stopped you, grabbed your hand and said, "Dance with me." At first you sort of swayed slightly to the 2 & 4 downbeat and then, as if the spirits were speaking to you, we both were pulled into a meditative dance to sounds of the Nyabinghi drums.

I wrote a poem about you. *Remembering Mom* was inspired by our reggae dance, by your cocoa brown skin, by the card that told me that you loved me the best way that you could.

Remember the nights we danced to reggae rhythms
And the days I bathed your brown-skinned beauty
Not because of any sense of duty
But because I knew those moments would be
The ones that showed you love
I will remember those moments, Mom.

Love,
Debra Ann

ABOUT THE CURATORS

Iresha Picot, M.Ed, BSL is a Licensed Behavior Specialist, and has a Master's Degree in Urban Education Policy and Post-Graduate work in Women Studies from Temple University. In addition to a Master's Degree, she has Post-Graduate certifications in Applied Behavior Analysis and Autism. Currently, Iresha works in the Behavior and Mental Health fields as a Licensed Behavior Specialist and Outpatient Therapist and is currently a Lead Clinician in a School Therapeutic Treatment program. Iresha is also a Birth Doula and a Prison Abolitionist.

Vanessa Hazzard is a Licensed Massage Therapist, writer, and healing arts educator from Philadelphia, PA. She has had her poetry and narratives featured in *Elephant Journal, For Harriet, Recovering Yogi, and Apiary Magazine's The Hive* and has been featured on *Newsworks.org* for combining activism with yoga and healing arts. She is currently earning her Bachelors in Applied Science from Siena Heights University and carries various group wellness certifications, including Yoga for Trauma & Addiction from the Transformation Yoga Project. Living with bipolar disorder, Vanessa aims to educate wellness professionals on mental illness by developing continuing education courses in depression, PTSD, and trauma-informed massage therapy.

Currently, Vanessa and Iresha are developing programming for trauma survivors which includes teaching a variety of coping skills (meditation, yoga, bodywork, writing, etc.) in small group settings. A portion of the funds from this book will be used to offer scholarships for this program to help people with low or no income.

For more information or to contact us:
www.pocmentalhealthnarratives.com.

RESOURCES

The resources provided are purely suggestions. They are not a substitute for medical care or meant to diagnose.

How to be a #Hoodtherapist in Your Own Home

By Iresha Picot

My Instagram handle is " @ireshadahoodtherapist". I gave myself that moniker because I spend the majority of my day as a therapist in one of Philly's most impoverished neighborhoods. I always say that bearing witness to people's struggle is my super power. And that is one half of my role, but in reality, my role is to empower families to work through their own issues and problems once my services are no longer needed. The behavioral and mental health system has never been on the side of the people; especially people of color. I always encourage the caregivers of the children in which I service as a therapist and behavior specialist to become their own active [hood] therapist in their home.

One of the fundamental breakdowns I find with the families is that there is a lack of communication and family-building that exists inside of the home. Families pass by each other to get to the television, video games, and to their phone. This creates more of a separation between the family, rather than bringing the family together as a strong family unit.

Below are several activities to assist you in facilitating open communication in your homes with your children.

Encourage and Utilize "Stop and Think" techniques.

S-Stop **T**-think **O**-Observe **P**-Plan/Proceed
T-is it true? **H**-is it helpful? **I**-Is it Inspiring? **N**-Is it Necessary? **K**-Is it Kind?

One Microphone

When having family conversations, encourage 1 microphone use at a time. This means that one person speaks at a time, while the other members of the family listens.

Skittles: "Candy Go Around"

Materials: Skittles.

During this game, the parent or child distributes 10-15 pieces of skittles to each person playing. Each person sorts their candy out by color with instructions not to eat them. Each color should represent a question or statement to answer. You can come up with your own statements or questions. Suggestions are below:

Green: Describe 1 to 3 things about yourself.

Purple: Name 2 positives and negative thing about your week.

Orange: Name a future goal and how you will attain it.

Red: What are 1-2 things you constantly worry about and why?

Yellow: List aspects of things you want to change about your family.

Stress Balls

Materials: Rice or sand, and balloons.

Cover a table or your floor with paper. Have one person hold the balloon, while the other person pours in the rice or sand. Do not fill to the top and tie the balloon at the end. Keep them around the house, so that when you or the child becomes stressed, they can grab a stress ball to de-escalate all angry or frustrated feelings.

Coping Skills Bingo (see additional handout in this book)

Create bingo cards that have several coping skills across the board (i.e. take deep breaths, keep a positive attitude, go for a walk). Create questions of instances where the children would have to utilize their coping skills (i.e. someone stepped on your new sneakers, or your father was recently arrested). With every question or scenario, the child will have to cover up a coping skill they will use on their bingo cards.

Vision Boards

Materials: Magazines, poster board, crayons, pencils

A vision board represents or symbolizes the experiences, feelings, and possessions you want to attract into your life, and place them in your board. Have your children create vision boards and goals for themselves, by using magazine cut outs and drawing pictures, words and signs on the boards. Encourage everyone in the family to make a collective vision board for the family.

No Judgment Hop Scotch:

Materials: Chalk

Draw a hopscotch outline outside on your sidewalk. Use chalk to draw a hopscotch pattern on the ground or use masking tape on the floor. Create a diagram with eight sections and number them. Use a penny or stone to throw into the outline. Remind the child/ren that whatever they want to share while playing this game is judgment free and they should be open to tell you as the parent, whatever they wish to share. If the person lands in "1", they have to tell the other person one thing that the other person does not know about them, if they land in "2", they have to tell two things, and so forth with the rest of the numbers.

Blowing Bubbles

Buy bubbles, and allow yourself and your children to blow bubbles when someone becomes angry or frustrated. Every time you are blowing a bubble, you are taking a deep breathe to calming yourself.

Therapeutic Hot Potato

Pass the "hot potato" around. When it stops on you, you have to give someone in the circle a positive comment or affirmation. A hot potato can be any light item that can be easily thrown around.

Dunking

Materials: A bowl, water and paper

As a group, write all the negative things you do not like about yourselves on individual sheets of paper. Remind them that only they have to look at the papers and no one else. Take turns dunking them into the bowl of water, in which the papers will dissolve. Also remind them that this is a symbol of washing away all the things that they do not like about themselves. Distribute new sheets of paper, where you and the children can write positive things you like about yourselves and steps to work towards retaining the positive aspects instead of the negative ones.

Board Games

Play board games to teach your children how to take turns amongst themselves and to simply spend time around each other.

Keychain Affirmation Rings

Materials: Key chains, cardstock, hole puncher and markers

Affirmations are positive and affirming statements. On each small piece of cardstock, you and the children will write positive affirmations that will encourage all to move forward in life, (ex. "I am beautiful and amazing"). After each person has written between 5-7 affirmations on cardstock, punch holes in the corner of the cardstock and loop on the key rings. Your children can keep these key rings with you in school and work.

Gratuity Lists

Write lists of all of the things that you are grateful for having/experiencing.

Toss and Talk Ball

Get a regular ball. On different spots of the ball, write different questions on it. Then have the children form a circle. When the ball is thrown to you, you have to read one question on the ball and answer it. After you finish it, you will then toss it to someone else.

Sharing the Load

Create a behavioral/task chart. Each child gets 1-2 (or more tasks) to do for the week to help free some time up for the caregiver. If they complete the task with satisfaction, reward them weekly with a small gift of their liking to reinforce the tasks at hand. This builds up a collective working unit in the home.

Cultural Life Maps

Have your children draw a road on paper with a beginning and ending point. The beginning of the road represents the beginning of their lives and the end, the future. Ask them to "map" out the most significant events that have shaped them as a person. Include important family members, significant experiences, etc.

More tips

- Be nurturing, comforting and affectionate.
- Talk with your children.
- Discuss expectations for behavior.
- Protect your children.

Always remember to give your children

RESOURCES

Books/Articles

Bahrampour, T. Therapists say African Americans are increasingly seeking help for mental illness http://www.washingtonpost.com/local/therapists-say-african-americans-are-increasingly-seeking-help-for-mental-illness/2013/07/09/9b15cb4c-e400-11e2-a11e-c2ea876a8f30_story.html (accessed June 2015)

Brown, Diane. (2003). In and Out of Our Right Minds: The Mental Health of African American Women. Columbia University Press; 1st edition.

Cabrebra, Natasha. (2011) Latina and Latino Children's Mental Health. Praeger/ABC-CLIO.

Ford, Matt. America's Largest Mental Hospital Is a Jail. http://www.theatlantic.com/politics/archive/2015/06/americas-largest-mental-hospital-is-a-jail/395012/ (accessed June 2015).

Head, John. (2010). Black Men and Depression: Saving our Lives, Healing our Families and Friends. Harmony Press.

Huebner, D. (2006). What to Do When You Grumble To Much. Magination Press of the American Psychological Association.

Metzner, Jeffrey. Solitary Confinement and Mental Illness in U.S. Prisons: A Challenge for Medical Ethics, J Am Acad Psychiatry Law 38:1:104-108 (March 2010)

Mather, C.L. (1994). How Long Does it Hurt? A Guide to Recovering from Incest and Sexual Abuse for Teenagers, Their Friends, and Their Families. Jossey-Bass

Rothschild, B. (2010). 8 Keys to Safe Trauma Recovery: Take-Charge Strategies to Empower Your Healing (8 Keys to Mental Health). W. W. Norton & Company; 1 edition

Vanzant. I. (2001). Yesterday, I Cried. Celebrating the Lessons of Living and Loving. Touchstone; 1st edition

Ward, Earlise. African American Women's Beliefs About Mental Illness, Stigma, and Preferred Coping Behaviors. Res Nurs Health. 2009 Oct; 32(5): 480–492.

Wright, L.B., & Loiselle, M.B. (1997). Back On Track: Boys Dealing with Sexual Abuse. Safer Society Press

Healing the Hurt: Trauma-Informed Approaches to the Health of Boys and Young Men of Color (PDF)

file:///C:/Users/Iresha/Downloads/Drexel%20-%20Healing%20the%20Hurt%20-%20Full%20Report%20(1).pdf

Early Childhood Trauma (PDF)

http://nctsn.org/sites/default/files/assets/pdfs/nctsn_earlychildhoodtrauma_08-2010final.pdf

Changing Places: How Communities will improve the Health of Boys and Colors (PDF)

http://technologylink.typepad.com/files/chapter-13-trauma-informed-practice-corbin-et-al..pdf

Souls of Black Men: African American Men Discuss Mental Health (PDF)

http://www.consumerstar.org/pubs/Souls.pdf

Podcasts

http://www.thisamericanlife.org/radio-archives/episode/484/doppelgangers?act=2#play

For decades, the writer Alex Kotlowitz has been writing about the inner cities and the toll of violence on young people. So when he heard about a program at Drexel University where guys from the inner city get counseling for PTSD, he wondered if the effect of urban violence was comparable to the trauma that a person experiences from war. Kotlowitz talks to a military vet from Afghanistan and a guy from Philadelphia who's lived in some pretty bad neighborhoods to find out if they are doubles of some sort.

Alex's is the author of the book 'There are No Children Here' and producer of the documentary film The Interrupters. (23 minutes)

To Head Off Trauma's Legacy, Start Young (NPR)

http://www.npr.org/sections/health-shots/2015/03/09/377569414/to-head-off-traumas-legacy-start-young

NPR "All Things Considered" story on March 9 about how health care providers can provide early intervention and services for families whose health may be affected by trauma.

Behind Mental Health Stigmas In Black Communities

http://www.npr.org/2012/08/20/159376802/behind-mental-health-stigmas-in-black-communities

Therapy APPS

Breathe2Relax

Sometimes, all we need to de-stress is take a few deep breaths. Created by the National Center for Telehealth and Technology, this app teaches users how to do diaphragmatic breathing. Features include educational videos on the stress response, logs to record stress levels, and customizable guided breathing sessions. (Free; iOS and Android)

eCBT calm

Implementing some of the many strategies of cognitive behavioral therapy, this app helps users assess their stress levels, practice mindfulness and relaxation skills, and connect their thoughts to feelings and behaviors. The end result is more calm in your everyday life and more awareness of your actions and emotions. ($0.99; iOS)

Happify

Want to kick negative thoughts, nix worry, and dial down stress? The array of engaging games, activity suggestions, and gratitude prompts makes Happify a useful shortcut to a good mood. Designed with input from 18 health and happiness experts, Happify's positive mood-training program is psychologist approved. Even cooler? Its website links to bonus videos that are sure to make you smile. (Free;

How Are You

Tracking your moods can help you fight the blues and teach you to tune into positive things. That's the premise behind this app. But as a bonus, it also allows you to compare your mood with worldwide averages, see which emotions you feel the most, and export your mood tracking data so you can share it with a mental health professional or trusted friend. ($9.99-$12.99; iOS and Android)

MindShift

This straightforward stress management tool helps users re-think what's stressing them out through a variety of on-screen prompts. At the same time, the app encourages new ways to take charge of anxiety and tune into body signals. (Free; iOS and Andriod)

Operation Reach Out

This mood tracker and resource locator was designed by Emory University researchers to aid in suicide prevention. The setup is simple: Users create a personal profile that includes emergency contact information, current medications, safety plans, and reminders for appointments or medications. Plus the app uses GPS to locate mental health care services nearby, should any user enter crisis mode. (Free; iOS and Android)

PTSD Coach

If you suffer from PTSD symptoms, this 24-hour tool that's linked directly with support services is a valuable thing to download. Available as an app or on the Web, PTSD Coach lets users select the specific issue they want to deal with (from anxiety and anger to insomnia and alienation), and then gives them guidance on how to lift their mood, shift their mindset, and reduce stress. (Free; iOS and Android)

Worry Watch

We all get anxious only to realize later our anxieties were overblown or irrational. The idea behind Worry Watch is to nip these moments in the bud. This app enables users to track what kick starts their anxiety, note trends in their feelings, observe when the outcomes were harmless, and keep tabs on insights to stop future freakouts. To lower your anxiety even further, Worry Watch is password protected—so whatever you divulge in the diary feature is safe and sound. ($1.99; iOS)

Adverse Childhood Experience Trauma checklist

http://www.hawthorncenter.com/wp-content/uploads/2015/06/ACE-Questionnaire.pdf

Coping Skills Bingo

B	I	N	G	O
Eat Healthy	Talk to a good friend	Understand how you feel	Go for a walk	Paint
Keep a positive attitude	Take Deep Breathes	Exercise	Think of a happy memory	Perform a random act of kindness
Play a Game	Use a Stress Ball	Free Space	Laugh	Dance
Sing	Watch your favorite movie	Journal	Talk to a trusted friend	Go for a Walk
Cry	Blow bubbles	Count from 1-10	Listen to your favorite music	Draw

Created by Iresha Picot

Coping Cards: Coping statements are truthful positive statements used to replace the negative and untrue thoughts that take-over when you feel anxious, stressed, angry and/or when facing other overwhelming situations. Since it is difficult at times to remember coping statements in stressful situations, it is always helpful to write them down to keep them with you. *(coping cards created by Iresha Picot)*

Cognitive Coping Cards

When I feel _____

I can do this instead:

1. _____

2. _____

Cognitive Coping Cards

I am proud of myself when:

1. _____

2. _____

3. _____

Cognitive Coping Cards

The next time I am in a bad situation in a relationship, instead of doing _____

I can:

    1. _____

    2. _____

    3. _____

Cognitive Coping Cards

I am more than capable of:

1. _____

2. _____

3. _____

CPSIA information can be obtained
at www.ICGtesting.com
Printed in the USA
LVHW082312280822
727055LV00002B/162